VICTORIAN LIFE

A VICTORIAN CHRISTMAS

KATRINA SILIPRANDI

Wayland

VICTORIAN LIFE

A VICTORIAN CHRISTMAS

A VICTORIAN FACTORY

A VICTORIAN HOLIDAY

A VICTORIAN SCHOOL

A VICTORIAN STREET

A VICTORIAN SUNDAY

VICTORIAN CLOTHES

VICTORIAN TRANSPORT

HOW WE LEARN ABOUT THE VICTORIANS

Queen Victoria reigned from 1837 to 1901, a time when Britain went through enormous social and industrial changes. We can learn about Victorians in various ways. We can still see many of their buildings standing today, we can look at their documents, maps and artefacts – many of which can be found in museums. Photography, invented during Victoria's reign, gives us a good picture of life in Victorian Britain. In this book you will see what Victorian life was like through some of this historical evidence.

This edition published in 1994
by Wayland (Publishers) Ltd

First published in 1993 by Wayland (Publishers) Ltd,
61 Western Road, Hove, East Sussex BN3 1JD, England

© Copyright 1993 Wayland (Publishers) Ltd

British Library Cataloguing in Publication Data
Siliprandi, Katrina
  Victorian Christmas. - (Victorian Life Series)
  I. Title II. Series
  394.20941

HARDBACK ISBN 0-7502-0718-3
PAPERBACK ISBN 0-7502-1371-X

Printed and bound in Great Britain by B.P.C
Paulton Books

Series design: Pardoe Blacker Ltd
Editor: Sarah Doughty

Cover picture: Christmas tree and children's musical instruments.

Picture acknowledgements
Bridgeman Art Library 4, 6 (top); ET Archive *cover*; Mary Evans 6 (bottom), 7 (both), 9, 10 (both),11, 12, 14 (both), 16, 17 (top), 18, 21 (bottom), 22 (top), 23, 24, 25, 26 (both), 27; Illustrated London News 15 (bottom); Mansell Collection 5, 13, 15 (top), 22 (bottom); Wayland Picture Library 19 (photographed by Paul Seheult).

Thanks to Norfolk Museums Service for supplying items from their museums on pages 8, 17 (bottom), 20, 21 (top).

All commissioned photography by GGS Photo Graphics.

CONTENTS

CHRISTMAS
HOLIDAY

What does Christmas mean to you? You will know it is the time for a school holiday, even if you do not celebrate Christmas. Christians have celebrated the birth of Jesus at Christmas time for nearly 2,000 years. But the modern form of the celebrations is quite new. When Queen Victoria's reign started in 1837, nobody had heard of Santa Claus or Christmas crackers. No Christmas cards were sent, and many people did not have a holiday.

EARLY FESTIVALS

For thousands of years, people all over the world have had midwinter festivals. Since Christianity came to Britain, these midwinter festivals have become mixed with Christmas celebrations. Even at the beginning of Victoria's reign, people in different parts of Britain celebrated various saints' days between 1 November and 2 February. The celebrations were often outdoors and involved everyone in the area. Dressing up in costumes was sometimes part of the festival.

A festival in Tudor times.

VICTORIAN CHRISTMAS

A family enjoying games on Christmas Day.

By the middle of the nineteenth century, it was becoming usual for middle-class people to see Christmas as a time for families to be together at home. Above, is a picture of a middle-class family enjoying Christmas in 1849. Families like this celebrated Christmas over two days, Christmas Day and Boxing Day. These middle-class ideas about Christmas began to spread to poorer people around Britain.

CHRISTMAS IN THE WORKHOUSE

This picture on the right shows people in Victorian Britain who have no home. The only place they could go to for food and shelter was the workhouse. On Christmas Day, special food was served in the workhouse. The people were given small gifts and they probably went to a carol service.

Homeless people on the streets at Christmas.

By 1880, most children aged between 5 and 10 went to school. At school they heard how richer people celebrated Christmas. Adults read about Christmas in newspapers.

A CHRISTMAS STORY

This picture comes from a book written by Charles Dickens. The story is called *A Christmas Carol*. It is about a man called Scrooge who is mean and cruel. This picture comes from the part of the story where he is shown the fun and jollity of a Christmas ball. By the end of the story he sees that he has been wrong and becomes kind and generous.

This book was very popular in Victorian Britain. It encouraged richer people to give money and gifts to the poor at Christmas time.

Mr Fezziwig's Christmas ball.

BOXING DAY

In this picture we see a rich woman bringing a hamper of gifts to a poor and elderly person. Victorian newspapers had many reports of charitable acts at Christmas, traditionally on Boxing Day. Gifts of food, money, clothes and small presents were made to orphans, poor families and old people. Parties were held for children.

In Victorian Britain, some people who lived in the country had to go to towns for work. The growth of railways meant that they could travel home to their families at Christmas. This was made easier from the 1870s when more places of work made Boxing Day a holiday.

A gift hamper.

CHRISTMAS IN THE EMPIRE

Some British people lived or worked in different parts of the British Empire in Victorian times. They tried to have the same sort of celebrations as middle-class families in Britain. This is a picture of people out hunting in India. They are eating a Christmas pudding as part of their meal.

In some parts of the world it is midsummer in December. Victorian families in Australia would probably have been outside having a Christmas picnic in the sun.

A Christmas hunting trip in India.

CHRISTMAS
AND THE CHURCH

Do you go to church on Christmas Day? Victorian families often went to church on Christmas morning. After they opened their Christmas stockings, they would usually walk to church or make the journey by horse-drawn coach. When they arrived, they would find the church was warm and decorated for Christmas.

Lighting the stove.

INSIDE THE CHURCH

This is a church on Christmas Eve. The stove is being lit to make sure that the church will be warm inside. The church is decorated with evergreen plants, like holly and ivy which do not lose their green leaves in winter. For centuries, evergreens have been used as part of midwinter festival decorations. Before Christianity, people thought that these plants were magical, so they hung them up to protect themselves from evil spirits and to encourage the spring to come. Christians gave new meaning to these old customs. For example, the prickles on holly reminded people that Jesus had worn a crown of thorns when he died.

A family at home at Christmas.

A FAMILY PARTY

People who lived in the country gathered evergreens from the trees and hedges. In towns, evergreens were bought in markets. People used evergreens to decorate their homes as well as their churches. Look at the decorations in the picture above. Can you see the mistletoe hanging from the oil lamp? There is also holly around the picture frames.

Parties like this would have been held in England and Wales on Christmas Day, but not in Scotland. In Scotland, Christmas Day did not become a holiday until long after Queen Victoria's reign and most children went to school as usual.

SINGING IN CHURCH

Churches in England and Wales were decorated like this at Christmas time. Many churches in Scotland were not decorated for Christmas as many Scottish people did not think that it was right to celebrate Jesus's birth with customs that had started long before Christianity.

These children are singing a Christmas carol. Carols were sung before Queen Victoria's reign, but few of them were written down. Victorian people collected and published many old carols. They also wrote new ones. Look at pages 28-9 of this book to find out when some carols were written.

A family at church.

CAROL SINGERS

During Queen Victoria's reign, singers and musicians visited houses at Christmas time. They were called 'the waits'. They sang carols and collected money. In the country they might be given a drink made from warm ale, apples and spices.

Most churches had musicians to accompany the carol singing in 1837. A writer called Thomas Hardy described a church band playing at Christmas time. He wrote 'Old William Dewy, with the violoncello, played the bass; his grandson Dick the treble violin; and Reuben and Michael Mail the tenor and second violins'.

'The waits', or musicians who play carols at Christmas.

Later most churches had organs or harmoniums instead of a band. At Inverness in Scotland, children went from house to house singing for four or five evenings before Christmas. They collected pennies and were called 'bulliegeizers'.

After the church service.

CHRISTMAS MATINS

Most middle-class Victorians went to matins on Christmas morning. This was the church service at 11 o'clock. Sometimes servants would also go to matins although often they were too busy preparing the Christmas dinner. They would go to church earlier in the morning instead.

CHRISTMAS
COOKING

Do you eat chicken or turkey sometimes? In Victorian Britain, white meat was too expensive for most people to buy. Some poor people did not eat anything special for Christmas dinner. In the north of Britain, roast beef was popular. People in the south often ate goose. Many poor people only had cheap meats to eat on Christmas Day. The main meats served on Christmas day in 1840 to Queen Victoria, her family and friends were beef and roast swan.

Collecting meat from the baker's oven.

THE BAKER'S OVEN

Many poor people did not have an oven. They took their goose, or other meat, to the baker's oven to be cooked. Look at the picture on page 12. Can you see how they kept the meat hot on the way home from the baker's shop? Working people saved a small part of each week's wages to pay for their Christmas goose.

Taking the pudding from the copper.

COOKING IN THE COPPER

Charles Dickens described Christmas pudding as a 'speckled cannon-ball'. It was shaped like a ball because it was wrapped in a piece of cloth to cook. Sometimes the pudding was cooked in the copper. A copper was a copper bowl, mounted in brickwork and was heated by a fire underneath it. Normally a copper was used to heat the water for washing.

CHRISTMAS WISHES

When the Christmas pudding was being made, each member of the family gave it a stir. As they stirred they made a wish. Silver coins were dropped into the mixture. Brandy was poured over the cooked pudding and lit. The flaming pudding was brought to the dinner table. Everyone hoped that their piece of pudding would have a coin in it, as this was lucky.

Stirring the pudding.

FOOD AT CHRISTMAS

At Christmas banquets, some rich people served boar's head. Eating boar's head was a custom from long before Christianity. Can you see what was put into the boar's mouth?

Turkeys were brought to Britain from America about 300 years before Queen Victoria's reign started. In early Victorian times, turkeys were walked from the farm where they were raised, to the poultry market in London. They sometimes wore small leather boots to protect their feet. It could take four months for the turkeys to travel from Norfolk to London. Later it was more usual for the turkeys to be killed on the farm and then brought to market by stage-coach.

The boar's head.

CHRISTMAS DINNER

The family in the picture below are enjoying Christmas dinner. In a rich household this was a magnificent feast. There would be a cook, kitchen maids and scullery maids to help to prepare the Christmas dinner, and do the washing-up. Less wealthy people might have their dinner around a large kitchen table, or if they were poor they might eat their food out in the street, straight from the baker's shop.

A meal on Christmas Day.

TWELFTH NIGHT CAKE

This was the cake made for Queen Victoria in 1849 on 6 January, which was Twelfth Night. In many parts of Victorian Britain this was a time for celebrations. As festivities around Christmas Day became more important, people stopped making Twelfth Night cakes. They made smaller cakes for Christmas Day instead. In Scotland, shortbread was made at Christmas.

Queen Victoria's Twelfth Night cake.

CARDS AND DECORATIONS

Do you send and receive Christmas cards? Today, millions of greetings cards are sent and received at Christmas. We also send greetings cards to celebrate festivals such as Easter or Diwali, or special occasions like birthdays or weddings. At the beginning of Queen Victoria's reign, however, Christmas cards were unknown.

THE FIRST CHRISTMAS CARD

One of the first Christmas cards was possibly made for Sir Henry Cole in 1843. He had a thousand cards like this one printed to sell in his art shop in London. Can you see what is happening in each of the three pictures? The cards cost a shilling each which was very expensive. At first Christmas cards were not very popular.

Sir Henry Cole's Christmas card.

NEW YEAR CARD

Early Victorian cards were usually greetings for New Year. Before 1840, the cost of posting a letter depended on how far it had to travel. The letter was paid for by the person who received it, not by the sender. In 1840, the Penny Post was introduced. People could buy a penny stamp to pay for the postage of a letter to anywhere in Britain. The Penny Post encouraged people to send cards. One penny was still quite expensive so poor people did not send cards.

A greetings card for New Year.

CHRISTMAS CARDS

New methods of printing were introduced later in Queen Victoria's reign. This made cards cheaper. A half-penny rate of postage was available from 1870. By then post could travel all over Britain by railway. Many more people sent Christmas cards. There were thousands of different cards. The pictures on them did not always have anything to do with Christmas!

A range of Christmas cards.

TREE AT WINDSOR CASTLE

Christmas trees were another new idea in Victorian Britain. This custom came from Germany. It was made popular in Britain by Queen Victoria's German husband, Prince Albert. He had a Christmas tree at Windsor Castle from the 1840s.

It soon became popular among wealthy people to buy a Christmas tree and decorate it with sweets, toys and fruits. In the 1880s, Christmas trees were often decorated with Union Jacks and the flags of the British Empire. Candles were put in metal holders on the tree and lit. In rich houses, a servant guarded the tree to make sure it did not catch fire.

The Christmas tree at Windsor Castle, 1848.

DECORATIONS

Many people made their own Christmas decorations. This decoration is called a kissing bough. Victorian families made these from wire or metal hoops. They were decorated with evergreens, fruit, ribbons, paper and a sprig of mistletoe. An old custom was to kiss under mistletoe.

Children made decorations by sticking strips of paper together with glue made from flour and water. They also made mottoes or messages of greeting, like 'A hundred, thousand welcomes' or 'A happy Christmas'. The words were cut from paper or made from evergreens. Poor people sometimes wrote Christmas messages with chalk around their fireplaces.

A kissing bough.

CHRISTMAS PRESENTS

Are you sometimes given toys as Christmas presents? At the beginning of Queen Victoria's reign children had few toys. Most toys were handmade by toymakers and were very expensive. Later, some toys were made in factories but they were still too expensive for poorer families to buy. From the 1870s, middle-class parents could buy games, books, dolls, Noah's arks and clockwork toys for their children.

TOYS

At the beginning of Victoria's reign, some adults gave each other presents on New Year's Day. Later it became more usual to exchange gifts on Christmas Day and for children to be given presents. From the 1870s, young children from richer homes spent much of their time in the family's nursery with a nursemaid. Games and toys like these would have helped to fill the time.

A selection of children's presents.

HANDMADE GIFTS

Many Christmas gifts were hand-made. Victorian magazines had ideas for presents to make. For example, children could make 'slippers for grandpapa, a pincushion for grandmama, mittens for papa, a photograph frame for mamma, a pen-wiper for a brother or an apron for a sister'.

In Scotland, it was said that 'though there were no Christmas cards and no decorating of churches, it was the custom at that season to make little gifts for all one's friends, relations and servants'.

Some beautiful hand-made Victorian gifts.

TREE PRESENTS

In rich families, children and servants were often given gifts from underneath the Christmas tree. Servants received useful presents. Sometimes they were given cloth to make into a new dress or shirt. This was the only present many poor people who worked as servants had at Christmas time.

Children collecting presents from the tree.

CHRISTMAS STOCKINGS

From 1870, many children hung up stockings on Christmas Eve. Rich children found them filled with toys on Christmas morning. Poorer children would have found presents in their stockings too – an apple or orange, a new penny and, perhaps, a small toy. Cheap toys were bought by poorer people from street traders or penny bazaars.

SHOPPING FOR GIFTS

Many Christmas gifts sold in shops were advertised in newspapers and magazines. After about 1880, middle-class people bought some of their presents from mail-order catalogues. Rich people chose their gifts at the shops and had them delivered to their homes. Sometimes the shopping was delivered by train. The porter brought it from the station to the rich person's house. After 1885, boys on bicycles often delivered shopping in towns.

Typical mail-order catalogue.

Presents for everybody.

FATHER CHRISTMAS

Ideas about Santa Claus, or Father Christmas, are a mixture of two stories. Before Victorian times, Father Christmas was part of midwinter festivals. Old stories describe him dressed in green – perhaps a sign of the returning spring. The other story was about St. Nicholas, known as Sinter Klaas in Holland.

Some Dutch people went to live in North America in the seventeenth century. They took the story of Sinter Klaas with them. From about 1870 their stories became known in Britain, where Sinter Klaas became Santa Claus. He had reindeer, a sleigh and toys for children. This story became mixed up with the British Father Christmas.

CHRISTMAS ENTERTAINMENTS

Do you enjoy the special programmes on the television at Christmas time? In Victorian Britain there was no television, so people made many of their own entertainments at home by playing festive games. Like children today, Victorian children also enjoyed visiting pantomimes which started on Boxing Day.

PLAYING GAMES

At Christmas time Victorian families enjoyed playing games. These children are playing Snapdragon on Christmas Eve. Brandy was poured over a bowl of currants. Then the brandy was lit. The players took turns to snatch currants from the flames and put them in their mouths. This was a dangerous game, so don't try it at home as you could burn yourself. Why do you think the game was called Snapdragon?

Playing Snapdragon.

FESTIVE GAMES

'Blind man's buff' was a favourite Victorian game. One person was blindfolded. This person had to find someone else and touch them. If you were caught you had to put on the blindfold. Charades were popular in Victorian Britain. Words are chosen and acted out. The people watching have to guess the words. Sometimes complete plays were acted by members of rich families. They dressed up and spent a great deal of time and money on costumes.

CRACKERS

After Christmas dinner, richer Victorian families enjoyed pulling Christmas crackers. Crackers were invented by Tom Smith, a London sweet maker, in 1846. The idea was copied from the French bonbons. These were sweets that were wrapped in a twist of coloured paper. Tom Smith added love notes to the bonbons to help to sell them. Then he had the idea of making the sweets go bang. His fire-cracker sweets were successful. He sold even more when he added paper hats and small toys.

Children pulling a Christmas cracker.

MAGIC LANTERN

Often Victorian families enjoyed a magic lantern show at Christmas time. Glass slides with pictures painted on them were put into the magic lantern. This had an oil lamp and lens in it. The picture appeared much bigger on the screen or on the wall. People in workhouses were sometimes entertained by a magic lantern show on Christmas Day. Many people did not have time for entertainments at Christmas. Servants, post office and railway workers had to work as usual.

A family being entertained by a magic lantern show.

MY FIRST PANTOMIME

There is a good description of a late Victorian middle-class Christmas in a book called *Jeremy* by Hugh Walpole. It says, 'There followed the Stockings, the Waits, the Carols, the Turkey, the Christmas Cake, the Tree, the Presents, Snapdragon, Bed...' The book continues, 'Although Christmas Day was over, Jeremy was very much looking forward to his first visit to the pantomime which started on Boxing Day. '

Pantomimes were popular treats for richer families in Victorian Britain. Some people had work at Christmas helping with the pantomime scenery. Others walked around the streets wearing boards that advertised the pantomime.

The fun of the pantomime.

TIME LINE

1830s

1837 Queen Victoria's reign begins.

1840s

1840 Penny Post introduced by Rowland Hill. Prince Albert puts up a tree at Windsor Castle.

1841 *Punch* magazine recommends people to be generous at Christmas.

1843 The carol, *O come all ye faithful* is translated from Latin.
The book *A Christmas Carol* by Charles Dickens is published.
Sir Henry Cole's Christmas card is produced.

1846 First Christmas cracker is invented by Tom Smith.

1848 Mrs. Alexander wrote the carol *Once in Royal David's City*.

1850s

1851 The carol, *See Amid the Winter's Snow* is published.

1860s

1868 The carol, *O Little Town of Bethlehem* is published.

1000			1500	1485	1603	1714	1837	1901	2000

1066 — MIDDLE AGES

NORMANS — TUDORS — STUARTS — GEORGIANS — VICTORIANS — 20TH CENTURY

1870s

1870 Half-penny rate of postage introduced for postcards.

1871 Christmas Letter Mission begins. The Mission sent a Christmas greeting to people in hospitals, workhouses and prisons.

1877 A poem by George Sims called *In the workhouse: Christmas Day*, is published.

1880s

1880 Service of Nine Lessons and Carols introduced by Bishop Benson at Truro, Cornwall.

1881 Christmas Letter Mission sends out 300,000 letters.

1883 The carol, *Away in a Manger* is published in the USA.

1890s

1891 The poem, *The Night before Christmas* by Clement Clarke Moore is published in Britain.

1894 Santa Claus Distribution Fund begins. The Fund gave presents and clothing to poor children.

1898 Turkeys become popular for Christmas dinner.

1900s

1901 The manufacturer Hornby invents Meccano. The toy industry begins to grow, and more toys were made in factories.

Queen Victoria dies.

GLOSSARY

Bass A large stringed instrument, played with a bow. It plays the lowest notes.

Boxing Day 26 December. It was the day servants and working people opened the boxes in which they had collected gifts of money.

British Empire Parts of the world once ruled by Britain.

Carol A dance or song of joy. By Victorian times it meant a Christmas religious song.

Charity The act of giving money or gifts to people poorer than yourself.

Christianity The religion of people who follow the teachings of Jesus Christ.

Christmas pudding A pudding usually made mainly from wheat flour, dried fruits, spices and beef fat.

Diwali A five-day religious festival celebrated by Hindus and Sikhs in the autumn.

Hamper A large basket with a lid, for carrying food.

Harmonium A musical instrument with a keyboard, like a piano. The player pumps air with foot-operated bellows. This air plays pipes like a miniature organ.

Mail-order catalogue A magazine you can choose gifts from, which are delivered.

New Year's Day 1 January, the first day of the New Year.

Novelties Small toys, ornaments or trinkets.

Orphan A child whose parents are dead.

Pantomime Theatrical entertainment. A pantomine has scenery, songs and dancing, often based around a children's story.

Penny bazaar Shops or market stalls where every item costs a penny.

Saint A holy person in the Christian religion.

Scullery A room for rough kitchen work like washing-up and peeling vegetables.

Shilling Twelve old pennies. Our modern equivalent is the 5p coin.

Street traders People who sell goods from a tray, basket or barrow in the street.

Tenor A viola, a stringed musical instrument played with a bow. It is about the same shape as a violin, but a little bigger. It plays low notes.

Twelfth Night A time that remembers the twelfth evening after the birth of Christ, when it was thought that the three Wise men visited Jesus in the stable.

Violoncello A stringed instrument rather like a violin, only larger and with lower notes. It is played with a bow and often called a cello.

Waits One of the old names for the singers and musicians that went from house to house at Christmas time.

Workhouse A place for poor, sick and old people who could not provide for themselves.

BOOKS TO READ

Bentley, D. *Christmas* (Wayland, 1988)

Blackwood, A. *Christmas* (Wayland, 1984)

Egan, L.B. *A Christmas Stocking* (Simon and Schuster, 1988)

Hunt, R. *The Oxford Christmas Book for Children* (OUP, 1981)

Reeve, J. (ed.) *The Christmas Book* (Heinemann, 1972)

Winstanley, R. *The Oxford Merry Christmas Book* (OUP, 1987)

Willson, R.B. *Merry Christmas: Children at Christmastime Around the World* (Heinemann, 1983)

Wood, T. *Christmas* (A & C Black, 1991)

PLACES TO VISIT

Many museums have special exhibitions, displays or reconstructions about Christmas. The museums listed below nearly always have a Christmas display in the winter, but telephone first to make sure:

ENGLAND

County Durham: North of England Open Air Museum, Beamish Hall, Beamish, Stanley, DH9 ORG. Tel. 0207 231811

Derbyshire: Sudbury Hall, Sudbury, Derbyshire. Tel. 0283 585 305

Humberside: Cusworth Hall, Cusworth Lane, Doncaster, Humberside. Tel: 0302 782 342

London: Bethnal Green Museum of Childhood, Cambridge Heath Road, London, E2 9PA. Tel. 081 980 2415

Gettrye Museum, Kingsland Road, London, E2 8EA. Tel. 071 739 9893

Victoria and Albert Museum, Cromwell Road, South Kensington, SW7 2RL. Tel. 071 938 8500

SCOTLAND

Lothian: Museum of Childhood, High Street, Edinburgh. Tel. 031 225 1131

WALES

Gwynedd: Museum of Childhood, Menoir Bridge, Anglesey. Tel. 0248 712498

INDEX